DIETS TO

A specialist in the natural sound dietary advice and those suffering from this problem.

DIETS TO HELP DIABETICS

by

MARTIN L. BUDD
D.O., M.R.O., Lic.Ac.

THORSONS PUBLISHERS LIMITED
Wellingborough, Northamptonshire

First published 1983
This edition revised and reset 1984
Second Impression 1985

© MARTIN L. BUDD 1983

*This book is sold subject to the condition that it shall not, by
way of trade or otherwise, be lent, re-sold, hired out, or
otherwise circulated without the publisher's prior consent
in any form of binding or cover other than that in which
it is published and without a similar condition including this
condition being imposed on the subsequent purchaser.*

British Library Cataloguing In Publication Data

Budd, Martin L.
    Diets to help diabetics.— Rev. and reset ed.
    1. Diabetes — Diet therapy
    I. Title
    616.4'620654 RC662

    ISBN 0-7225-1137-X

Printed in Great Britain by
Richard Clay (The Chaucer Press) Ltd,
Bungay, Suffolk

CONTENTS

INTRODUCTION

This small book has been written for the diabetic sufferer. Many books on diabetes are available (a selection is listed under *Recommended Reading* on page 61) dealing with every aspect of diabetes including history, cause and control. There is, therefore, little point in repeating subjects that are well covered elsewhere. It is my intention to review the central problem for the diabetic, namely, food selection, with an additional emphasis on natural whole foods, vitamins and minerals of special value to the diabetic, and to give further information on various diets for the different types of diabetes.

The majority of books written for the diabetic describe food essentially as a balancing agent between the blood sugar and insulin production. Unfortunately little has been written describing the nutritional requirements of the diabetic, not only in terms of blood sugar stability but also in terms of the special needs created by diabetes and diabetic complications.

It has been estimated that approximately 25 per cent of diabetics are treated by diet alone, a further 25 per cent by insulin and diet, and the remaining 50 per cent are treated by diet or oral hypoglycaemic agents (sulphonylurea compounds). These figures serve to emphasize the important place that correct diet has in the treatment of diabetes. Not all forms of diabetes are permanent. In some cases there is a reversibility factor and, although variable, this factor applies in particular to the acquired diabetic (i.e. a person who acquires diabetes from adolescence onwards). However, the so-called inherited diabetes can also respond to correct nutritional programmes. Second only to the control of blood sugar is the need to counteract the long-term complications associated with diabetes. This aspect of treatment which involves the taking of natural substances as dietary supplements will be covered in Chapter 6.

It is perhaps appropriate that food is central to diabetic control, for the diabetic is, to a large extent, his own doctor. He is required to monitor his urine sugar at regular intervals, to know and understand the relationship between food, insulin and exercise. Moreover, he is obliged to achieve this balancing act on a day-to-day basis or suffer the consequences. There are few illnesses that require this level of patient participation and understanding.

Diabetes has been termed 'the prosperity disease', as it is often linked with overeating. It is virtually unknown in poorer countries, but where refined Westernized food is eaten to excess up to 3 per cent of the population are afflicted. In Great Britain, for instance, there are 1½ million diabetics. It is therefore no surprise that 80 per cent of diabetics are overweight prior to diagnosis, and food quality and quantity is a vital aspect of diabetic control.

Many patients are presented with a diet sheet, a prescription for drugs or injections and advised to avoid sugar for the rest of their lives. Individual dietary needs are rarely discussed. Lack of understanding by the patients often leads to discouragement and boredom coupled with a sense of frustration for, although the blood sugar when treated is soon within the accepted normal range, the patient still has diabetes and there is little being done to improve his general health. Dieting almost by definition is boring and any imposed regime, after several weeks, can reduce incentive. The diabetic is obliged to adhere to a precise diet for the rest of his life. If, however, the diet has purpose and variety it becomes much easier to follow and the rewards are greater.

This book is not a self-treatment manual, and the advice offered should be adopted in the context of any current medical treatment or medical supervision. I do not attempt to offer an alternative programme to the orthodox medical approach to diabetes, but rather a more natural elaboration or extension of the hospital diet. One can only generalize when discussing the nutritional needs for the diabetic patient, as no two sufferers are exactly alike. Readers are therefore advised to consult a qualified naturopath or nutritionally orientated doctor to obtain individual guidance on dietary requirements.

CHAPTER 1

THE DIABETIC DIET

The non-diabetic usually holds the simplistic view that diabetics need to avoid sugar and all will be well. This attitude perhaps stems from the belief that diabetes is a condition of high blood sugar entirely caused by insulin deficiency. Unfortunately, as with many diseases, diabetes does not involve one simple imbalance, for when there is any disturbance of the blood constituents many systems of the body are usually affected. The consumption of *all* the food groups affects the blood sugar in various degrees, for fats and proteins can also be partially converted to glucose. The ideal diabetic diet needs to fulfil six main requirements:

1. Blood sugar control.
2. Weight control.
3. Foods for health.
4. Catering for special needs.
5. The minimizing of complications.
6. The provision of variety with economy.

1. Blood Sugar Control
The priority requirement for any diabetic diet is the need to assist blood sugar balance by achieving and maintaining the blood glucose level within an acceptable range. This essential control is only possible when the other factors of exercise and treatment are also considered. Whether the prescribed diet

recommends a high fat or high carbohydrate emphasis or includes supplementary vitamins and minerals, the prerequisite should always be blood sugar control; all else is secondary to this essential requirement.

When we speak of blood sugar levels we mean the amount of glucose in the blood. Glucose is a simple sugar and is the end product of a digestive chain that begins by eating sugar (carbohydrate) or by eating protein or fat. Glucose is one of the chief fuels of the body and it is further broken down into carbon dioxide and water with the release of energy. To prevent an inappropriate increase in the blood sugar the body has several safeguards, including the release of insulin. Conversely there are also safeguards to prevent the blood sugar dropping too rapidly, including the release of adrenaline. There is, therefore, a balance between several opposing processes, and diabetes should be seen as a disturbance of the total blood sugar regulating mechanism rather than simply an insulin deficiency. Conversely, the opposite of diabetes — low blood sugar — is rarely caused by a simple insulin excess. It is therefore important to look at diabetes as a total health problem rather than the unfortunate effects of one malfunctioning gland.

2. Weight Control

Many workers and specialists dealing with diabetes recognize that obesity is the main causative factor in diabetes. Obesity is a word that has attracted many euphemisms including bonny, plump, tubby, chubby, nicely rounded, etc. This has probably come about (as do most euphemisms) because many people are unwilling to label themselves — or want to be labelled — obese. In fact they prefer not to think of 'obese' as describing grossly fat but simply nicely plump. This rationalization, although very human, contributes to a situation in Western nations where 20 per cent of the population is obese.

Contrary to the popular belief that our weight should ideally increase as we grow older, we should in fact lose weight with age. The body's efficiency in terms of muscle strength, joint and bone integrity, circulation and digestion all reduce or slow down with age, and any weight is an extra burden. Excessive eating (especially of refined carbohydrate and sugar-rich foods) leads to inappropriate demands on the body's sugar regulating apparatus, and the pancreas may become exhausted and underactive. Unfortunately the refining of cereals and other foods has created a situation where our appetite control is by-passed. In natural more primitive conditions sugar is not refined and is only found in certain fruits, vegetables and grains. Consuming such foods in their natural state ensures that we cannot eat a great deal of sugar as the absorption rate is naturally controlled by quantity.

It is probable that excessive consumption of refined sugar is the cause of the diabetic explosion in the last half century in the so-called civilized nations. Paradoxically there are also underweight diabetics. These are usually young sufferers prior to receiving therapy. Usually, weight loss is the result of insulin deficiency which causes the body to break down valuable tissue for use as fuel. Insulin facilitates the storage of starch and fat. This particularly applies to the acquired diabetic in middle age who is receiving insulin injections. The simple avoidance of carbohydrates cannot redress the balance in the blood sugar. The complete and safe breakdown of fats requires the presence of a limited amount of carbohydrate in the diet. Furthermore it should be noted that even fats (10 per cent converted) and proteins (56 per cent converted) are partially converted to glucose. It would therefore be necessary to avoid all foods to prevent sugar entering the bloodstream. When diabetics avoid all carbohydrates they often lose weight and develop ketosis (acidosis). The underweight diabetic is therefore encouraged to include more carbohydrate in his diet, at the same time keeping a careful watch on his urine sugar readings.

It is wrong to assume that extra fat (which is usually acquired by a high calorie diet) is safely stored away in muscle tissue. The muscles do indeed act as storage depots, but surplus fat is also stored in the liver, eventually leading to an overloading of the body's sugar and fat metabolism apparatus. This can contribute to many conditions one associates with obesity, including heart and circulation problems, strokes, high cholesterol levels, narrowed arteries, digestive and bowel problems, varicose veins, ulcers and accelerated joint wear and, of course, diabetes. The effect of excess weight in diabetes is not difficult to understand, and the diagram summarizes the vicious circle that may result from overeating and high blood sugar.

Unfortunately there is a tendency with insulin-dependent diabetics to match their carbohydrate allowance to their insulin dosage rather than the more important considerations of weight and general health. This situation is partly

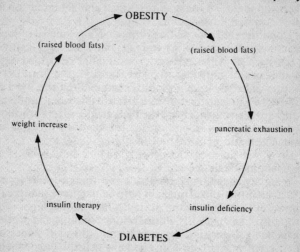

Obesity and diabetes

caused by an understandable fear of 'hypoing' (a term used to describe a sudden fall in blood sugar or hypoglycaemia brought about by an inappropriate insulin excess). This is often caused by too fine a balance between the insulin dosage and food consumed which may be disturbed by undue exercise, stress, illness, etc. A slight rise in the blood sugar can occur without producing symptoms, but a fall in the blood sugar can give rise to very distressing symptoms including palpitations, dizziness, sweating, breathlessness and even collapse. With this in mind many insulin-dependent diabetics prefer to eat too much refined carbohydrate to balance their insulin dose, thus safeguarding against the possibility of a hypo effect. This has several drawbacks, but in the context of weight the most obvious is that many sufferers have a high calorie, high carbohydrate diet with an unnecessarily high insulin dosage to match.

Paradoxically the usual treatment for a hypo effect is to

prescribe glucose tablets. The diets and menus in later chapters provide alternatives to the orthodox approach to the diabetic diet with the twofold purpose of blood sugar control and general health building with weight loss. If this is achieved there can in many cases be a gradual reduction in the dependence on insulin.

Insulin has been termed 'the fattening hormone' because it assists the storage of fat and starch. This consideration presents a persuasive case for treating diabetics without insulin, or with minimal insulin and nutritional support. As a starting point the weight should be normalized and the diet should be planned to avoid future weight increase. One of the tragedies of diabetes is that the diabetic needs to keep slim, yet he is often dependent on a substance that increases fat storage.

3. Foods for Health

Any discussion on diabetes tends to be obsessed with sugar, yet to use a nutritional metaphor, this concern over sugar can be a red herring. Many diabetics, upon diagnosis, are introduced to sugar substitutes, calorie counting and special diabetic foods, yet little attention is paid to food values or food supplements. The assumption is that the only area in which a diabetic's diet differs from the normal diet is the avoidance of sugar and the need to keep a careful eye on carbohydrates. Some authorities do not feel this to be the case and believe the diabetic's requirements are such that his need for vitamins, minerals and other nutrients is far in excess of those of the so-called healthy individual. The diabetic's ability to assimilate, store and utilize certain substances is usually impaired and he may also have an inherited predisposition that creates a requirement for certain food components greatly in excess of the average.

The diabetic should pay special attention to whole grains, alternative natural sugar, chemical-free foods and organically grown fruits and vegetables, also additive-free healthy meat, plant proteins and dietary fibre. If this is done there may be effective blood sugar control without excess weight, and a general improvement in health and vitality with fewer complications. An important aspect of the correct diet for the diabetic is the question: 'What is the optimum carbohydrate-fat ratio?' This is one of the main sources of controversy in the treatment of diabetes, and the key to this argument is an understanding of what is meant by fats and carbohydrates, and what would be considered a natural balance between the two. To look for clues it is necessary to consider the variety and amount of fats and carbohydrates eaten by primitive diabetes-free peoples. This important topic will be covered later, with a comparison of the various diets in current use.

4. Catering for Special Needs

The maintenance of a normal level of blood sugar depends on the availability of many interacting substances within the body. If these components, including hormones, enzymes, vitamins and minerals are lacking or deficient, or in some instances in excess, then diabetes may be the result. The essential biochemical balance of many of these substances is influenced by a great number of factors including our diet, inheritance, past health, stress and certain drugs (including alcohol, caffeine and tobacco). It would be quite wrong to regard diabetes as simply the consequence of a failing pancreas. The pituitary gland, thyroid gland and the adrenal glands all influence blood sugar metabolism, and partial removal of the thyroid gland in hyperthyroidism has been known to alleviate diabetes by raising the insulin levels. In addition oestrogen, which has an antagonistic effect on insulin, can also encourage high blood sugar. The liver also plays its part in blood sugar control, having the capacity to store excess sugar (as glycogen), and to release the stored sugar into the blood when needed. Liver damage due to disease, alcohol or drug abuse may disturb this delicate control and lead to a sugar build-up in the bloodstream.

You will see that the fight against diabetes should not be billed as 'insulin versus sugar'. The key to blood sugar balance is the availability of a great number of minerals, vitamins, trace elements and amino acids for these are the building blocks for the hormones and enzymes that regulate our blood sugar metabolism. The only source of these vital components is the food we eat. The diabetic has special dietary needs for certain substances that may not be adequately supplied in the normal diet. Having talked about the individual needs of the diabetic it may be of value to delve a little deeper into the special nutritional requirements created by diabetes. We are all individuals, not only in terms of personality and fingerprints. We are also biochemically unique. An essential aspect of medical research and drug prescribing has been the need for standardization. The identification and classification of what constitutes the 'average', whether applied to the blood pressure, height, weight, body type, organ size or blood constituents, and the commonly agreed 'normal ranges' are necessary for the diagnosis, definition and treatment of many diseases. Unfortunately the word 'average' has become confused with, and is frequently used to define, the normal and this can be very misleading and inaccurate.

The main drawback in recognizing normal ranges as a diagnostic aid is that it excludes the possibility of individual variations outside the range. As an example, the average person may need 30mg of vitamin C daily to maintain normal health and avoid scurvy symptoms, yet many people with a poor health history or an inherited need for large amounts of vitamin C may require 2,000mg to attain the same effect. It follows that if such people only obtain 30mg from their diet they would probably develop symptoms of vitamin C deficiency. In other words, vitamin, mineral and other deficiencies are often a development of our own individual biochemical needs, and the recognition and correct treatment of individuality should take priority over rigid adherence to normal range requirements.

This is a vast subject that cannot be fully covered here, for many nutrients are known to relate to the cause and treatment of diabetes. The more important of these are discussed in Chapter 6. Many diabetics need, and greatly benefit from, vitamin and mineral supplements properly prescribed and monitored, but as this is not an area that can be recommended for self-treatment professional advice should be sought.

5. The Minimizing of Complications
The need for special vitamin and mineral-rich foods in the diabetic diet is of special relevance when preventing and treating the many long term complications to which the diabetic is prone. Quite apart from the more obvious symptoms of diabetic coma or insulin shock (brought on by too little or too much insulin), many diabetics develop retinitis, cataracts, fatty livers, peptic ulcers, obesity, high cholesterol

levels and circulatory impairment leading to ulceration, gangrene, strokes, high blood pressure and heart attacks. Although all these complaints also occur in non-diabetic patients the incidence of many of these is far higher in diabetics.

A contributory cause of these distressing complications is the loss of essential water-soluble vitamins and minerals via the urine in diabetes. Saccharine, and many other sugar substitutes, and tobacco all serve to reduce vitamin C availability. (The amount of vitamin C lost with each cigarette smoked is around 25mg or 1g lost for 40 cigarettes.) The nutritional requirements for these substances is therefore many times greater than for the non-diabetic. The levels of many of the B vitamins, vitamin C, potassium and other minerals are further reduced by the stressful effects of blood sugar fluctuations. When a sufferer 'hypos', or develops acidosis, the adrenal compensation creates a greater need for these substances. Likewise, protein requirements are also raised when the adrenals are stimulated.

You will begin to see why the diabetic needs super nutrition to compensate for these health destroying factors. The commonly held view that a Western diet provides all our nutritional needs falls down badly when applied to the diabetic. The combined factors of blood sugar imbalance, altered fat metabolism and the high urine loss of vital nutrients creates deficiencies that can only be rectified by a diet tailored to the diabetic's individual needs and health history. This should include 'emphasis foods' which are foods rich in certain recommended vitamins and minerals, and supplements in the form of additional vitamins and minerals.

6. The Provision of Variety with Economy
Eating should be a pleasure, and well cooked, well presented food is usually enjoyable to eat. The diabetic diet, however, could easily become dull and boring. The challenge to the diabetic, therefore, is to find a varied diet with plenty of wholesome food at an acceptable price that also fulfils his blood sugar needs. Proteins and 'health foods' and special diabetic foods are usually expensive, yet many rarely-used plant proteins, carbohydrates and whole grains are readily available and inexpensive. This important topic — variety in foods — is not always covered in hospital diets, but it is an

important area as wholegrains and plant foods, being
complex carbohydrates, are especially rich in the vital
nutrients so needed by the diabetic. To advocate exotic fruits
and best quality meats as routine dietary items would be
pointless and unhelpful, yet there are many foods, particularly fruits, grains and vegetables that are rarely considered
by the British housewife. When cooking for a diabetic it is as
well to remember that his condition automatically excludes
many foods and drinks that form a major part of the normal
diet. It is essential, therefore, to look for more variety in
foodstuffs, particularly as many less common foods are of
special value to the diabetic. The diet section later in the book
deals with little used yet valuable foods.

CHAPTER 2

REVIEW OF
CURRENT DIETS

Considerable controversy surrounds the question: 'What is
the ideal diet for a diabetic?' With the great knowledge we
now possess of the biochemistry of the body the concept of a
standardized, generally prescribed diabetic diet should be
unanimously accepted. Unfortunately this is not so. There
are many different diets prescribed and every few years new
theories are developed that claim to form the basis for the
perfect diet. Although all the various programmes set out to
control the blood sugar, the manner in which this control is
achieved and the type of foods recommended show enormous and often conflicting variety. The main area of
contention is the proportion and quantity of the three main
food groups, i.e. fats, carbohydrates and proteins. With this in
mind it is worth briefly describing examples of the four main
diabetic diets in current use.

The Traditional Diet

Before insulin was isolated and prescribed in the 1930s it was
normal to treat diabetes with a very high fat, low carbohydrate diet. The rationale behind this kind of diet was the
assumption that if the diabetic was unable to metabolize
sugar, owing to an insulin deficit, then it was only sensible to
avoid all forms of sugar. The more extreme programmes
allowed for a daily total of 7-8oz of fat and only 1-2oz of
carbohydrate. This diet was difficult and expensive to follow,
and in the pre-insulin era only delayed the inevitable early
death associated with uncontrolled diabetes; for whilst we
can avoid eating sugar we cannot avoid sugar (as glucose)
passing into the blood. Both proteins and fats can also be
partially converted into glucose. Fortunately, this type of diet
is now rarely prescribed, as a greater understanding of animal
and vegetable fats and carbohydrate foods has served to
highlight its shortcomings. However, the high fat diet has its
modern counterpart in what some American nutritionists
call the ketogenic diet.

Ketogenic Diet — High Fat, Low Carbohydrate

The chief proponent of this type of diet is Dr Robert C.
Atkins who advocates restricting carbohydrates (to 5 per cent
of the diet) and increasing the fat/protein content. Dr Atkins
argues that diabetes, except for the juvenile inherited insulin-
dependent variety, should be seen as the second part of a
progressive disease involving the blood sugar, the first part
being hypoglycaemia — or low blood sugar — caused by an
overworked pancreas. The majority of acquired diabetics do,
in fact, have a history of hypoglycaemia with symptoms
including obesity, migraine, fatigue and sugar cravings. Dr
Atkins maintains that a low carbohydrate diet slows down the
progress of the disease by relieving the exhausted pancreas
and claims that the condition, when treated in this way,
improves to a state of 'remission'.

The diet is designed to deliberately create ketosis or
acidosis. This means that, when the dietary carbohydrate is
reduced to a very low level, the stored fat (triglyceride) and
the fat in the diet become the major fuel sources in place of
glucose. The triglyceride breaks up into the two fuels, free
fatty acids and ketone bodies, hence the name 'ketogenic
diet'. When these substances are detectable in the blood the

person is said to be in a state of ketosis. Dr Atkins does not consider this type of diet at all risky unless the diabetic is insulin-dependent and out of control. He does not see it as a danger to the stable non insulin-dependent diabetic. Physicians using this diet claim great success but opponents of the high fat regime claim their own successes.

High Carbohydrate/Low Fat Diet

By way of contrast, and to emphasize the dichotomy of thinking that prevails concerning diabetic diets, a high carbohydrate, low fat diet is also recommended by many diabetes experts. As much as 80 per cent carbohydrate is advised with approximately 13 per cent protein and 7 per cent fat. At first sight this proportion of carbohydrate seems absurdly high for a diabetic patient whose major problem is an inability to metabolize sugar. Yet great success is claimed with this diet and perhaps the key to its success is the importance placed on the *type* of carbohydrate that is recommended, namely wholemeal, high fibre grains, cereal products and vegetables and fruit. For this reason the diet is also known as the H.C.F. (high carbohydrate fibre) diet. This may seem extreme to many readers but the dietary programme outlined by Paavo Airola, the famous American nutritionist, goes a stage further.

American Airola Diet

To quote Dr Airola: 'Not only the overeating of sugar and refined carbohydrates, but also proteins and fats (which are transformed into sugar if eaten in excess) is harmful and may lead to diabetes. Too much food taxes the pancreas and paralyses its normal activity.' With the knowledge that diabetes is virtually unknown in poor countries the diet sets out to recommend the opposite of the typical Western diet. It is meatless, low caloried and high in raw natural foods. Approximately 80 per cent of the diet is raw with 4-5 small meals and no refined carbohydrate, the emphasis being on alkaline vegetables, fruit and milk products with a little unrefined carbohydrate in the form of millet, oats and other grains.

Each of these diets, different though they may be, is claimed to be very successful in the treatment of diabetes. It seems illogical that dietary regimes so opposed all work, and the only rational explanation for this is that the diets will all help a certain type of diabetes. This leads to the obvious statement that there cannot be one diet for all diabetics, and indeed diabetes falls into two major groups. It therefore follows that every diabetic diet should be tailored to individual needs, not simply in terms of the patient's weight, age and activity but the type of diabetes he suffers.

CHAPTER 3

DIETS TO HELP DIABETES

Medical research uses many methods to assess the value of a treatment whether dietary or drug therapy. These include single and double blind trials, laboratory testing with animals and analysis of blood and urine. There are, however, other ways in which the causes and effects of disease can be identified and evaluated without recourse to experiments and trials. This is simply to look at the history of a particular disease in relation to eating habits in different periods of history, and also to study the incidence of the disease in different countries and peoples. In this way environmental factors whether geographical, economic or dietary may be recognized. When diabetes is studied in the light of history and epidemiology (distribution of disease) several interesting facts come to light.

1. Primitive societies have a lower incidence of diabetes than civilized societies.
2. The incidence of diabetes does not seem to relate to food groups, i.e. high fat versus high carbohydrate, but more specifically the *type* of carbohydrate (refined versus unrefined) and the type of fat (unsaturated versus saturated).
3. Historically diabetes is on the increase. Being relatively rare in the last century, it is now almost epidemic and greatly on the increase in all Western nations.
4. Diabetes relates to affluence, the prosperous Western

nations having a far greater percentage than the less affluent so-called Third World countries.

Dr T. L. Cleave in his excellent book *The Saccharine Disease* deals very thoroughly with the relationship of diabetes to different cultures and diets. In particular he traces the incidence of diabetes in primitive cultures before and after the introduction of Western dietary influences (i.e. refined foods and sugar). There is also considerable evidence to show the close connection between diabetes and the consumption of sugar and sugar-rich foods. Graphs showing sugar consumption and diabetes incidence are remarkably similar. A clear appreciation of the ideal diabetic diet has been somewhat obscured for the last half century by the many nutritionists and physicians who have advocated either a high fat/low carbohydrate diet, or a low fat/high carbohydrate diet. Controversy also surrounds the question of which diet is suitable for what type of diabetic. Quite apart from considerations of calorie requirements it is quite obvious that an underweight prediabetic patient relying only on a diet for balance has totally different dietary requirements from the obese middle-aged insulin-dependent diabetic.

Many see the classification of diabetes into groups and subgroups as needlessly complex and serving only to confuse the patient. Let us look at the typical diabetes classification list and see if it can be simplified.

Classification of Diabetes
This is usually according to three factors:
1. Patient's age and onset of symptoms.
2. Treatment prescribed.
3. Degree of patient's own insulin production or availability.

Diabetic Types
1. Childhood diabetes.
2. Juvenile onset diabetes.
3. Maturity onset diabetes.
4. Diabetes of the elderly.

Childhood Diabetes. Also known as hereditary diabetes, this usually involves absolute insulin deficiency and usually requires insulin therapy for life.

Juvenile Onset Diabetes. This frequently occurs in the adolescent and is thought to be caused by a latent hereditary factor. Although this type of diabetes is thought to be insulin-dependent there is a potential reversibility factor that can respond well to natural therapy and correct diet.

Maturity Onset Diabetes. This type of diabetes is usually acquired by people prone to incorrect eating and other destructive habits. There is often a previous history of hypoglycaemia (caused by excess insulin stimulation) with sugar craving, migraine, fatigue and overweight. This type can usually be controlled by correct diet alone and/or oral drugs, as the insulin deficiency is only partial.

Diabetes of the Elderly. Essentially an extension or worsening of the maturity onset type, and is usually an expression of a gradually failing pancreas. There is also with increased age a greater incidence of complications.

As you will see from the groups that follow, there are, in fact, only two classes of diabetes, and these can be grouped as follows:

Childhood inherited diabetes
Juvenile onset diabetes } Juvenile diabetes

Maturity onset diabetes
Diabetes of the elderly } Adult diabetes

Some authorities go as far as to suggest these two groups are so different that they should be seen as separate diseases. This statement is not as provocative as it may seem for, although the signs and symptoms of the two diseases may be identical, the events leading to the eventual diabetes can be quite dissimilar.

Juvenile Diabetes
Although many children have an acquired proneness to blood sugar imbalance, diabetes should not be seen as a congenital abnormality. There is, of course, a strong genetic background in diabetes in young children, but it is suggested that the influence of personal make up and incorrect diet could be of more significance in the causation of diabetes than hereditary defects. The incidence of diabetes in young children is far greater than the incidence of any known congenital condition. Defects that occur in less than 5 per

thousand live births (i.e. spina bifida, cleft palate, club foot, Down's syndrome, etc.) contrast with the overall proportion for diabetes of 30 per thousand of population, although this figure includes the adult onset diabetes. Therefore, to attribute diabetes to congenital defects may be overlooking the true cause. Given that the juvenile diabetic may be born with an under-sensitive pancreas, a diet high in refined sugars may lead to a gradual underactivity and eventual diabetes. As many juvenile diabetics develop rapidly to an insulin-dependent state they are frequently underweight.

Diabetic parent or grandparent
↓
Child born with under-sensitive pancreas
↓
Pancreas vulnerable to refined sugars
↓
Tendency to weight loss
↓
Insulin deficiency
↓
Diabetes

Adult Diabetes

Many adult diabetics have a history of low blood sugar. This may seem a paradox, but a high sugar refined food diet can lead to overactivity followed by eventual exhaustion of the pancreas. This produces an insulin excess (causing low blood sugar) followed by a gradual insulin deficiency (diabetes). The phenomenon of overstimulation of a gland with subsequent exhaustion can be observed in other glandular problems, in particular the adrenals and thyroid. The adult diabetic who for years has abused his sugar-regulating system by taking excess coffee, alcohol and refined carbohydrate is often overweight, hence the obvious link between diabetics and obesity.

Many hypoglycaemia sufferers with symptoms of migraine, asthma, etc. find to their delight that in their late forties and fifties their symptoms gradually recede. This apparent improvement in their condition is an illusion, for as the pancreas becomes less efficient, their blood sugar swings from being too low to the diabetic situation of being too high.

This is a gradual process, usually over a period of several years, and many adult onset diabetics can be controlled with diet alone, or with diet and oral drugs, without recourse to insulin therapy. The element of reversibility is more pronounced than in the juvenile onset type. As the early stages of diabetes are usually symptom-free the migraine or asthma sufferer quite wrongly assumes that he is getting better. On the same theme many elderly diabetics have a past history of migraine or other hypoglycaemic symptoms.

Diabetic parent or grandparent
↓
Child born with over-sensitive pancreas
↓
Sugar craving and high sugar diet
↓
Tendency to gain weight
↓
Poor utilization of insulin due to excess fat
↓
Hypoglycaemia
↓
Diabetes

Summary

To summarize, the juvenile diabetic's condition is usually rapid in onset, insulin-dependent, and unstable (sometimes termed 'brittle'); he is also underweight. This is because the blood sugar-insulin balance becomes very sensitive, causing rapid fluctuations that are difficult to control. The adult or maturity onset diabetic is usually slow in onset, and can be controlled by diet or oral drugs. There is usually a tendency to be overweight with a history of low blood sugar. Adult diabetes is relatively easy to stabilize. The difference between the two types of diabetes is further highlighted by the tendency for adult diabetics to have a fat problem, frequently the cholesterol and/or triglyceride level in the blood is raised, and by mid-life the circulation is already beginning to show the symptom changes or complications associated with a high sugar, high fat build-up.

Treatment

The treatment for the two types of diabetes differs as follows:

Juvenile Diabetes. A moderate to high unrefined carbo-hydrate diet of approximately 2,000 Calories per day is ideal. This facilitates an improved sugar/insulin balance and helps to prevent sudden swings in blood sugar. This type of high carbohydrate diet also serves to increase weight. A low protein and low fat content is also recommended as excessive fats serve to reduce the diabetic's sensitivity to insulin, thus reducing its effectiveness. Too much fat, whether from animal or plant sources, may also create a state of ketosis which the young insulin-dependent diabetic cannot easily control. The correct carbohydrate/fat ratio should be 3-1 in favour of carbohydrates (including raw fruit and vegetables), and proteins (animal and plant) should make up the remaining 15-20 per cent.

Adult Diabetes. One of the most significant differences between the two types of diabetes is that the juvenile type usually has an absolute insulin deficiency whilst the adult's insulin availability is usually relative or partial. Indeed it has been shown that many adult obese diabetics have an *excess* of insulin in their blood brought about as a result of a high sugar diet which stimulates excessive insulin production. Unfor-tunately this high level of insulin cannot be utilized due to a high level of fat in the blood, thus creating high blood sugar. The adult diabetic tends to have a history of a high calorie, high sugar diet which has, of course, contributed to his diabetes. It is therefore appropriate to prescribe a low calorie moderate carbohydrate diet of around 1,200 Calories. This should have an emphasis on unsaturated fats and plant proteins and, as many adult diabetics have a raised blood cholesterol level, it is important to avoid cholesterol-rich foods, and include a high fibre content in the diet.

CHAPTER 4

CHOOSING YOUR DIET

The ideal diet for any diabetic should consist of unrefined, slow-digesting carbohydrates which require very little insulin for their metabolism and also contain a high fibre content. This applies in particular to millet, oats, beans and vegetables. An additional bonus obtained with oats and other whole grains is that it has been found that they can actually lower blood cholesterol. The chief difference between simple carbohydrate (sugar, etc.) and complex carbohydrate (grains, vegetables, etc.) is the absorption rate in the blood. With complex carbohydrates, that should be eaten 'as grown', the breakdown into glucose is slow, providing approximately two Calories per minute on a 3,000 Calorie diet throughout twenty-four hours. With simple sugars, however (and these never occur naturally), there is a glucose 'rush' of up to 100 Calories or more, with subsequent excessive swings in the blood sugar and insulin levels.

To avoid such swings and obtain optimum calories from food as a slow steady stream, the diabetic's diet should contain 60-80 per cent complex carbohydrate content, with 3-5 meals daily. The rapid absorption of simple sugars found in refined carbohydrates also permits us to eat a large number of calories. For example, the calorific value of 5 oz of chocolate is the equivalent of 3 lb of apples. (Quite obviously our appetite may permit us to eat the chocolate in a few minutes, but 3 lb of apples would be impossible to consume so rapidly.) The proportion of complex carbohydrate in the diet is dependent on the type of diabetes and, of course, the patient's weight. Just as the refining of food affects its absorption, so processing and cooking may reduce the food value. It is therefore essential to have at least one raw food meal daily.

Although fats and, in particular, animal fats have long been advocated for diabetes it is indisputable that they lead to raised lipid (fat) levels in the blood. Simple carbohydrates also contribute to this process as they are often eaten far in excess of immediate needs and, as a result, are converted and stored as fat. There is no real need for excess fat in our diet as many green vegetables and nuts have an 8-10 per cent fat content which is quite sufficient to fulfil the body's requirements of fat.

Choosing Your Ideal Diet

The concept of *choosing* a diet may seem strange to the diabetic sufferer who probably follows a prescribed standard hospital diet sheet. The key to diabetes control is flexibility, so the diet neeeds to be tailored to your individual requirements and life style. The main purpose of the diet must be blood sugar control achieved by a combination of correct diet, exercise and appropriate treatment. The next consideration must be the type of diabetes, for this determines such factors as carbohydrate-fat ratio, calories and, as will be covered in later chapters, the need for supplements and 'emphasis' foods.

Let us begin by outlining a typical day's menu for the juvenile and adult diabetic, remembering that the ideal meal plan is 5-6 meals daily. These need not be equal in size as the majority of people have three main meals daily. The solution is to have an additional supper, plus one or two snack meals mid-morning or mid-afternoon.

Juvenile Diabetic (2,000 Calories)

Breakfast:	whole grain cereal	2 oz (55g)
	skimmed milk	½ pt (285ml)
	orange	1
	wholemeal toast with vegetable margarine	1 slice
Snack:	apple	1
	or	
	Ryvita with vegetarian pâté	2 slices
	or	
	grapes	12
Lunch:	lean meat	2 oz (55g)
	potatoes (small)	2
	butter beans	4 oz (115g)
	carrots	4 oz (115g)

Dessert:
tinned fruit without sugar   ½ cupful

Snack: see above

Dinner: cold chicken breast   2 oz (55g)
                Ryvita with vegetable
                    margarine   2 slices
                brown rice   6 oz (170g)
                or:
                cold potatoes with   2
                    mayonnaise
                side salad consisting of
                    tomatoes, cress,
                    cucumber, lettuce

Snack: see above

Snack or   apple   1
Supper: *or:*
                Ryvita with vegetarian
                    pâté   2 slices
                or
                grapes   12

Adult Diabetic (1,200 Calories)

Breakfast: porridge   4 oz (115g)
                skimmed milk   ½ pt (285ml)
                grapefruit   ½

Snack: apple   1
                or:
                Ryvita with vegetable
                    margarine   1 slice
                or:
                skimmed milk   4 fl oz (115ml)

Lunch: open sandwich with
                2 oz (55g) lean ham
                or 2 oz (55g) pork
                or 4 oz (115g) cottage
                cheese on *Ryvita* or

wholemeal bread with
vegetable margarine.
Also lettuce, tomato, sliced
raw carrot or beet,
watercress with low calorie
dressing

Snack: see above

Dinner: grilled cod or plaice   4 oz (115g)
                  brown rice   6 oz (170g)
                  including two of the
                  following:
                  sweet corn, butter beans,
                  cabbage, onions or
                  broccoli   3 oz (85g)

                  Dessert:
                  small banana or pear   1

Snack: see above

Snack or   apple   1
Supper: *or:*
                  Ryvita with vegetable   1 slice
                     margarine
                  or:
                  skimmed milk   4 fl oz (115ml)

Food Choices

The diabetic needs to have a greater awareness of food values
and selection than the non-diabetic, for the diet is usually
based on a system of 'exchanges' or 'substitutes'. This works
as follows: foods and drinks are divided into 6-10 groups, e.g.
vegetables, cereals, fruit, meat, fats, etc. These are so planned
that all the items in each group have approximately the same
calorific value and food value in terms of protein, fat and
carbohydrate content. The value of this type of listing is
obvious: each meal can be planned by selecting a food from
each group (for instance, breakfast may consist of one of
cereal group, one of milk group, one of fat group and two of
fruit group). Although one food may be exchanged for

another on the same list, foods on one list may not be exchanged for foods on a *different* list.

This simple method of classifying food has several advantages over the tedious method of using one master list of recommended foods, and foods to avoid. The exchange system provides a daily calorie count, and the diabetic knows and controls the proportion of fat, protein and carbohydrate he consumes. Most important of all, variety is provided by such a comprehensive listing. The many authorities and specialists on diabetes all have their own method of classification, but whichever is followed it is always advisable to consult your own doctor before make any changes to your existing diet.

The concept of food exchanges was initially formulated in America in 1950 by a government committee when the following groups were recommended:

1. Milk and similar foods.
2. Vegetables.
3. Fruit.
4. Breads.
5. Protein.
6. Fats.

To allow for greater flexibility, particularly in carbohydrate selection, some specialists now recommend ten groups:

1. Milk.
2. Vegetable A (low calorie).
3. Vegetable B (middle calorie).
4. Vegetable C (high calorie).
5. Beans.
6. Cereal.
7. Bread.
8. Fruit.
9. Meat.
10. Fat.

Food Exchange Lists
Meat — Each exchange contains: 50 Calories
                                       8g protein
                                       2g fat
                                       0g carbohydrate

Beef (lean)	1 oz (30g)
Pork	1 oz (30g)
Ham	1 oz (30g)
Lamb	1 oz (30g)
Chicken	1 oz (30g)
Cod	2 oz (55g)
Plaice	2 oz (55g)
Haddock	2 oz (55g)
Trout	2 oz (55g)
Halibut	2 oz (55g)

Fat — Each exchange contains: 45 Calories
0g protein
5g fat
1g carbohydrate

Oil (all types)	1 teaspoonful (5ml)
Margarine	½ oz (15g)
Almonds	3 medium (10g)
Brazils	1 large (10g)
Peanuts (roasted)	1 tablespoonful (10g)
Walnuts	1 whole (1g)

Bread — Each exchange contains: 50 Calories
2g protein
0g fat
10g carbohydrate

Wholemeal bread	¾ oz (20g)
Rye bread	¾ oz (20g)
White bread	½ oz (15g)
Crackers	½ oz (15g)
Flour (wholemeal)	½ oz (15g)

Cereal (breakfast) —
Each exchange contains: 50 Calories
2g protein
0g fat
10g carbohydrate

Bran flakes	¾ oz (20g)
Corn flakes	½ oz (15g)
Puffed rice	½ oz (15g)
Porridge oats (dry)	½ oz (15g)
Weetabix	½ oz (15g)

Vegetables (These are divided into 3 carbohydrate groups)
  A — Each exchange contains: 13 Calories
                               1g protein
                               0g fat
                               2g carbohydrate

Asparagus	3 oz (85g)
Brussel sprouts	3 oz (85g)
Carrot	3 oz (85g)
Cauliflower	3 oz (85g)
Green peppers	3 oz (85g)
Marrow	3 oz (85g)
Onion	3 oz (85g)
Turnip	3 oz (85g)

  B — Each exchange contains: 24 Calories
                               2g protein
                               0g fat
                               4g carbohydrate

Beetroot	2 oz (55g)
Peas (fresh and frozen)	2 oz (55g)
Parsnips	2 oz (55g)
Swede	2 oz (55g)

  C — Each exchange contains: 55 Calories
                               2g protein
                               0g fat
                               10g carbohydrate

Potatoes (boiled or baked)	2 oz (55g)
Rice (raw)	⅓ oz (10g)
Spaghetti (raw)	½ oz (15g)
Corn (on the cob)	½ large cob

Free vegetables (These contain negligible carbohydrate and
can be used freely)

Celery, Courgette, Cucumber, Lettuce, Mushroom, Radish, Spinach

Beans — Each exchange contains: 65 Calories
5g protein
0g fat
10g carbohydrate

Baked beans (tinned)	3 oz (85g)
Broad beans	4 oz (115g)
Butter beans	2 oz (55g)
Haricot beans	2 oz (55g)
Kidney beans	2 oz (55g)
Lentils (soaked)	3 oz (85g)

Fruit — Each exchange contains: 40 Calories
0g protein
0g fat
10g carbohydrate

Apple	1 medium
Apricot (fresh)	3
(dried)	6 halves
Banana	1 small
Cherries (raw)	20
Dates (dried)	2
Figs (raw)	1 large
(dried)	1
Grapefruit	1 medium
Grapes	10
Peaches	1 medium
Pears	1 medium
Plums	3
Raisins	1 oz (30g)
Strawberries	15
Tangerine	2 small

Milk — Each exchange contains: 80 Calories
8g protein
0g fat
10g carbohydrate

Skimmed milk (liquid)	7 fl oz (200ml)
(powdered)	¼ oz (20g)
Natural yogurt	5 oz (140g)

CHAPTER 5

SAMPLE MEAL PLANS

Although the food exchange system to some extent simpli-
fies food selection for the diabetic there is still a need to
combine 3-4 exchanges for each meal and this can become
very tedious. For a variety of reasons, including lack of time,
habit and work conditions, we tend to be conservative in our
choice of meals. This particularly applies to breakfast and
lunch, whilst it is customary to include a greater variety in the
dinner or evening meal. Every country has a typical national
breakfast, and the British are no exception, but the first meal
of the day for many of us is simple, routine and brief.
Similarly, only limited time is allowed for our lunch break
and the meal usually lacks variety. For this reason I have
chosen to amend the usual exchange listings in favour of
several typical menus for breakfast and lunch for seven days.
The evening meal, or main meal of the day, can be selected
from the list of main protein foods on page 43. Should you,
however, wish to keep strictly to the 1,200 or 2,000 Calorie
diets, then recommended calories for each meal are
provided.

As a further guide to food selection, Chapter 6 deals with
'emphasis' foods, or foods of special value for the diabetic due
to their vitamin or mineral content. The accompanying
section on food supplements will serve to highlight the food
components so essential to the diabetic, whether assisting the
blood sugar stability or helping to minimize complications.
The meals are based on a 1,200 or 2,000 Calorie limit, which
can be adapted to the type of diabetes treated. Any variation
of calorific need may be worked out on an individual basis

using the diets provided. Variations will, of course, depend largely on your weight, treatment programme and level of activity.

The evening and lunchtime meals may be reversed, and the timing of snacks should be approximately mid-morning, mid-afternoon and just before going to bed. This combination of meals spread over 14-15 hours a day, consisting of complex carbohydrates and being low in protein and fats, allows for optimum slow absorption and energy availability.

SAMPLE MEAL PLAN (1,200 Calories)
BREAKFAST (160-170 Calories)
Content: Carbohydrate 70 per cent; Fat 15 per cent; Protein 15 per cent.

Day 1	Cornflakes, Shredded Wheat or Shreddies	½ oz (15g)
	Skimmed milk	6 fl oz (170ml)
	Orange *or* Apple	1
Day 2	Wholemeal toast with vegetable margarine	2 small slices
	Vegetarian pâté	
	Grapefruit	1
Day 3	Tomato juice	4 fl oz (115ml)
	Crispbread (wheat or bran)	½ oz (15g) or 2 slices
	Cottage cheese	3 oz (85g)
	Small apple *or* banana	1
Day 4	Porridge, including water	4 oz (115g)
	Raisins *or* grapes	10
	Skimmed milk	3 fl oz (90ml)
	Dried apricots	6 halves
	Prunes	5
Day 5	Poached egg	1 large
	Wholemeal toast	1 slice
	Grapefruit	½

Day 6	All Bran, Puffed Wheat	
	or Special K	½ oz (15g)
	Skimmed milk	6 fl oz (170ml)
	Stewed apple	1 oz (30g)

Day 7	Wholemeal toast	1 slice
	Cheddar cheese (toasted)	1 oz (30g)
	Tomato	1 slice

To drink: Any natural bottled mineral water. The waters with listed minerals are to be preferred, e.g. *Evian*. For variety, a *small* cupful of herb tea, e.g. rose hip or mint; or decaffeinated coffee.

LUNCH (220 Calories)
Content: Carbohydrate 70 per cent; Fat 15 per cent; Protein 15 per cent.

Day 1	Unsweetened apple juice	4 fl oz (115ml)
	Crispbread with vegetable margarine	2 slices
	Lean ham	2 oz (55g)
	Small tomato, lettuce & cucumber	

Day 2	Omelette with herbs	2 eggs (large)
	Apple, pear *or* banana	1

Day 3	Cottage cheese	4 oz (115g)
	Celery	2-3 sticks
	Fresh pineapple	4 oz (115g)
	or strawberries	4 oz (115g)
	Pumpernickel	2 slices
	or wholemeal bread	1 slice

Day 4	Chicken breast	6 oz (170g)
	Small tomato	1
	Cucumber, cress, lettuce, radish with low calorie dressing	
	Sliced orange *or* tangerine	1
	Crispbread with vegetable margarine	1 slice

Day 5	Wholemeal toast with vegetable margarine	1 slice
	Baked beans in tomato sauce	5 oz (140g)
	Small apple *or* pear	1
Day 6	Crispbread with vegetable margarine	2 slices
	Cheddar cheese	1½ oz (45g)
	Sliced raw pepper *or* onion	2 oz (55g)
	Sliced tomato	1
Day 7	Wholemeal bread with vegetable margarine	2 large slices
	Tinned salmon *or* tuna (oil drained off)	1½ oz (45g)
	Sliced cucumber	

Drinks as for breakfast.

SNACKS (3 daily, 80 Calories each = 240 Calories)
Content: Carbohydrate 70 per cent; Fat 15 per cent; Protein 15 per cent.

Snacks to be taken mid-morning, mid-afternoon and just before going to bed.

Small slice wholemeal bread *or* crispbread *or* 1 slice pumpernickel with scraping of vegetable margarine and one of the following:	1
Cottage cheese	3 oz (85g)
Hard boiled egg sliced	½
Vegetable pâté (Tartex etc.)	
Lean ham	1 oz (30g)
Chicken breast	1 oz (30g)
Sliced cucumber, lettuce, radish, cress may be added	

Further snacks include apple, pear, orange, banana, grapefruit, peach, apricot, 4 dates, 6 plums, 15-20 strawberries, 20 grapes, 25 cherries, handful of raisins, 6 fl oz (170ml) skimmed milk and 1 hard boiled egg. One of each constitutes a Snack.

DINNER (600 Calories)

Content: Carbohydrate 70 per cent; Fat 15 per cent; Protein 15 per cent.

To allow for greater flexibility the list includes only the main protein component. This amounts to approximately 250-270 Calories, the remaining 300-350 Calories to be allocated as follows:

1. Fruit juice or clear soup to
   commence the meal   40-60 calories
2. Rye bread, wholemeal bread, roll
   or pumpernickel to accompany
   the meal   60-80 calories
3. A selection of vegetables including
   potatoes and/or side salad   140-160 calories
4. Dessert: 1 piece of fruit   50 calories

Vegetarian meals: Vegetarian food may replace the meat providing it is not in excess of 300 Calories.

Drink as recommended for breakfast.

N.B. Condiments, pickles and sauces are discussed later in the book, Chapter 7.

Main Course Proteins (250-270 Calories)

Roast beef	4 oz (115g)	Lean steak	4 oz (115g)
Organ (offal) meats	4 oz (115g)	Chicken	5 oz (140g)
		Lamb	5oz (140g)
Turkey	5 oz (140g)	Cod	8 oz (225g)
Pork or ham	5 oz (140g)		
Haddock	8 oz (225g)	Halibut	8 oz (225g)
Sole	8 oz (225g)	Plaice	8 oz (225g)
Cooked brown rice	5 oz (140ml)	Wholemeal spaghetti	2½ oz dry weight (70g)
Corn on the cob	2 cobs	Cheese omelette	2 eggs
		Cheddar cheese	1 oz (30g)

SAMPLE MEAL PLAN (2,000 Calories)

BREAKFAST (360-400 Calories)

Content: Carbohydrate 70 per cent; Fat 15 per cent; Protein 15 per cent.

Day 1	Fresh orange juice	4 fl oz (115ml)
	Cornflakes, Shredded Wheat (R) or Shreddies (R)	1 oz (30g)
	Skimmed milk	8 fl oz (225ml)
	Wholemeal toast with vegetable margarine	1 slice
	Apple	1
Day 2	Tomato juice	4 fl oz (115ml)
	Plain goat's milk yogurt	4 fl oz (115ml)
	Pure bran	1 dessert-spoonful
	Grated apple or pear	1
Day 3	Grapefruit juice	4 fl oz (115ml)
	Scrambled egg	2 large eggs
	Wholemeal toast with vegetable margarine	1 slice
	Banana	1
	Raisins	1 dessert-spoonful
Day 4	Pineapple juice	4 fl oz (115ml)
	Porridge, including water	8 fl oz (225ml)
	Skimmed milk	4 fl oz (115ml)
	Dried apricot halves *or* prunes	8
	Pumpernickel or crispbread with vegetable margarine	1
	Vegetable pâté	1 oz (30g)
Day 5	Grape juice	4 fl oz (115ml)
	Wholemeal bread	1 slice
	Cheddar cheese (toasted)	2 oz (55g)
	Sliced tomato	1
	Orange	1
Day 6	Fresh orange juice	4 fl oz (115ml)
	Wholemeal bread with vegetable margarine	1 slice
	Baked beans	5 oz (140g)
	Poached egg	1
	Apple or pear	1

Day 7	Apple juice	4 fl oz (115ml)
	Crispbread with vegetable margarine	2 slices
	Cottage cheese	4 oz (115g)
	Swiss muesli (sugar-free)	2 oz (55g)
	Skimmed milk	6 fl oz (170ml)

LUNCH (380-420 Calories)

Day 1	Open sandwich with pumper-nickel or crispbread with vegetable margarine	2 slices
	Lean ham	4 oz (115g)
	Sliced tomato	1
	Fresh or unsweetened tinned pineapple	1 slice
	Sliced raw carrot	4 oz (115g)
	Potato salad with low fat mayonnaise	4 oz (115g)
	Cress, lettuce or cucumber if desired	
	Banana	1

Day 2	Steamed plaice or cod	6 oz (170g)
	Wholemeal bread (or roll) with vegetable margarine	1 slice
	Butter beans	2 oz (55g)
	Grilled tomatoes	4 oz (115g)
	Broccoli or courgettes	

Day 3	Goat's milk yogurt	5 oz (140g)
	Grated apple	1
	Rye bread with vegetable margarine	1 slice

Day 4	Cold beef	4 oz (115g)
	Jacket potato with vegetable margarine	2 oz (55g)
	Skimmed milk	4 fl oz (115ml)
	Mixed green salad	
	Orange	1

Day 5 Wholemeal bread with vegetable 2 slices (large)
        margarine
      Tinned or fresh salmon or tuna 2 oz (55g)
        (oil drained off)
      Sliced cucumber
      Apple or pear   1

Day 6 Egg mayonnaise consisting of   1
        hard boiled egg
        low fat mayonnaise and
        green side salad
      Wholemeal bread with vegetable 1 slice (large)
        margarine
      Cold baked beans   5 oz (140g)
      Grapes *or*   10-12
        plums   6

Day 7 Cold turkey or chicken (white   6 oz (170g)
        meat)
      Coleslaw with low fat dressing   2 oz (55g)
      Mixed green salad
      Skimmed milk   6 fl oz (170ml)
      Crispbread with vegetable   2 slices
        margarine

DINNER (800 Calories)
The main protein component of the meal should account for 270-300 Calories, the remaining 400-450 Calories to be allocated as follows:

1. Fruit juice or home made soup   50-70 Calories
2. Wholemeal bread or roll with   50-60 Calories
    first course
3. Potatoes or brown rice (4 oz/115g)   140-200 Calories
4. Vegetable and/or side salad   80-100 Calories
5. Dessert (fresh or sugar-free   100-120 Calories
    tinned fruit)

Drinks as recommended for 1,200 Calorie diet.

Main Course Proteins (270-300 Calories)

Lean beef	5 oz (140g)	Pork or ham	5 oz (140g)
Lamb	5 oz (140g)	Offal or organ meats	4 oz (115g)

Chicken and			
turkey (white)	6 oz (170g)	Cheese omelette	2 eggs
Spaghetti	4 oz (115g)	Cheddar cheese	1 oz (30g)
(wholemeal		Halibut	8 oz
dry)			(225g)
Haddock	8 oz	Sole	8 oz
	(225g)		(225g)
Plaice	8 oz	Cod	8 oz
	(225g)		(225g)

SNACKS (3 snacks at 120 Calories = 360 Calories)
As with the 1,200 Calorie diet these should be taken mid-morning, mid-afternoon and just before going to bed. The snacks for the 2,000 Calorie diet are very similar to the 1,200 Calorie diet except for the recommended amounts. The 2,000 Calorie allows for two slices of wholemeal bread, or crispbread, with the various ingredients. In addition to the recommended fruits, you can add 4-6 fl oz (115-170ml) skimmed milk or 4 fl oz (115ml) natural goat's milk yogurt.

Variety
These weekly charts are to be seen as guides for meal planning and need not be followed to the letter. There are, however, many meal permutations that can be worked out from the lists. In addition, equivalent proteins and snacks can be substituted to achieve greater variety.

CHAPTER 6

EMPHASIS FOODS AND SUPPLEMENTS

The expression 'emphasis foods' refers to foods that are rich in the vital nutrients so needed by the diabetic. These include many vitamins and minerals that are essential, and, for a variety of reasons already discussed, the diabetic needs a greater quantity of these than the non-diabetic.

There are two ways in which the diabetic can obtain these extra nutrients:

1. By ensuring that foods rich in these substances feature prominently and regularly in the diet.
2. By taking balanced and adequate amounts of these vitamins and minerals in the form of supplements.

Although it is often argued that we should obtain all our nutrients via our diet, the diabetic has special needs caused by his condition. All except the most severe or aged diabetic are likely, therefore, to benefit from a diet that is not only tailored to their type of diabetes, their weight and lifestyle, but also a diet that is rich in these vital nutritional components.

The notes that follow can be only a summary of this complex subject, but it should serve to provide 'food for thought'.

VITAMINS AND MINERALS OF SPECIAL VALUE FOR DIABETICS

Vitamin A
Diabetics are very susceptible to infections. One possible reason for this is their inability to efficiently convert beta-carotene, the commonest form of carotene, into Vitamin A. They can, however, utilize the Vitamin A found in animal sources, e.g. milk, fish livers, egg yolk, etc. — foods which they are generally advised to limit owing to their high fat content. Vitamin A supports the glands that help protect us from infection. These glands include the thyroid, thymus and adrenal glands. It is also of value in reducing blood cholesterol and maintaining the health of the eyes. This makes it especially valuable for diabetics.

The B Vitamins
This large family of water-soluble vitamins is essential in many areas of diabetic control. There are usually high urinary losses of all the water-soluble nutrients in diabetes, but the B vitamins are of special importance due to their wide ranging effects on the metabolism.

Vitamin B_1 (Thiamine)
The level of thiamine in the body is reduced by caffeine,

tobacco and other stimulants, also by excessive exercise and stress. It has been demonstrated that insulin production can be increased when this vitamin is provided in the diet. Large amounts of thiamine are also of value in treating acidosis and diabetic neuritis. The processing of many foods, in particular rice, flour and sugar, strips these foods of thiamine, providing more evidence to support the need for whole grains in the diabetic diet.

Vitamin B$_2$ (Riboflavin)

This is the vitamin that causes the urine to harmlessly turn bright yellow when we take Vitamin B Complex. As with thiamine, it has been shown to stimulate insulin production. 'Brittle' diabetics seem to derive particular value from it. The most important role of this vitamin is its intimate involvement with visual disorders. Lack of B$_2$ in the diet leads to a whole range of visual problems, an area of great risk in the diabetic.

Vitamin B$_3$ (Niacinamide, Nicotinamide and Nicotinic acid)

When there is mild deficiency of this vitamin there are psychological symptoms including anxiety, depression and anger. Insulin-dependent diabetics have an unusually high requirement for B$_3$, its value being in reducing insulin sensitivity in young diabetics; it also serves to prevent the sudden swings in blood sugar that are characteristic of this type of diabetes. Vitamin B$_3$ forms an important part of the Glucose Tolerance Factor (G.T.F.), an organic compound which assists insulin-glucose control (see under Chromium).

Pantothenic Acid (Calcium pantothenate)

This important member of the Vitamin B family is closely involved with the body's adrenal efficiency (cortisone and adrenalin production). When severe fluctuations in blood sugar trigger the diabetic's stress mechanism, pantothenic acid with Vitamin C and other nutrients are needed. With Vitamin B$_1$ and B$_2$ this vitamin is closely involved in insulin production and the level of cortisone in the body. For this reason pantothenic acid has been termed the 'anti-stress vitamin'. Fortunately it is present in many foods (the vitamin's name is derived from the Greek word 'pan' meaning 'all'). Unfortunately, approximately 50 per cent is lost in food processing and refining, e.g. the milling of flour causes 50-60 per cent loss.

Vitamin B$_6$ (Pyridoxine)

This is another B vitamin that is reduced through the diabetic's water loss. There is an increased need for B$_6$ with excess oestrogen, and deficiency symptoms have been observed in women taking the Pill. For this reason B$_6$ is of value in pre-menstrual tension. Deficiency of B$_6$ has been shown to cause pancreatic damage in animals and many workers point to lack of this vitamin as being a major contributory factor in diabetes. Tests have also shown that many diabetics lack Vitamin B$_6$ in their blood, suggesting that they may have a genetic need for this vitamin greatly in excess of that provided by a typical diet. Excessive production of urine owing to the diabetic's great thirst leads to a further depletion of the available B$_6$. In conjunction with Vitamin B$_2$ this vitamin has been known to improve diabetic retinitis.

Choline and Inositol (Lecithin)

These little-understood B vitamins are often linked as they are both closely involved with fat metabolism and combine to form Lecithin. The enlarged fatty liver of the diabetic can be partly attributed to the urinary losses of these two vitamins. The main role of Lecithin is cholesterol control and the absorption and transport of the fat-soluble vitamins A, D, E and K. As Choline and Inositol also assist in controlling high blood pressure, liver and gall bladder activity they are of great importance to the diabetic.

Vitamin B$_{12}$ and Folic acid

These two vitamins are biochemically connected and deficiency of either leads to anaemia. They have special value in fatigue, neurosis and the degenerative symptoms of old age. Vitamin B$_{12}$ is of special importance for the liver, and deficiency in B$_{12}$ can cause an increase in the blood sugar. When prescribed in conjunction with Lecithin B$_{12}$ assists fatty livers and fat metabolism generally.

Vitamin C

It has been shown that diabetics have a significantly lower level of Vitamin C in their blood platelets than normal

control subjects. As it is the excessive clumping or clotting of
platelets that contributes to atherosclerosis and other circulation problems it seems likely that taking supplementary
Vitamin C may be of value in preventing some of the
complications of diabetes.

Vitamin C acts as a detoxifier, reducing or negating the
harmful effects of lead, mercury, arsenic, carbon monoxide
and many drugs. The therapeutic effect on insulin is
increased in the presence of Vitamin C, while the side-effects
of many drugs (e.g. aspirin) can be reduced by taking this
essential vitamin.

The diabetic learns to dread infections; even the common
cold can throw his insulin-glucose level off balance. Vitamin
C is of proven value, not only in preventing simple infections,
but also shortening their duration. Although the recommended minimal daily requirement is 30mg Dr Linus
Pauling, the leading authority on Vitamin C usage, advocates
4-10g daily in order to reach blood saturation level. It should
be noted that approximately 50 per cent of Vitamin C intake
is lost through the urine by healthy persons; and far more is
lost by diabetics.

Vitamin E

To the diabetic, taking Vitamin E can be likened to taking out
insurance. The benefits of this vitamin are neatly
summarized by Dr Shute in his book *The Complete Updated
Vitamin E Book* in which he says: '. . . the reasons that alpha
tocopheral (Vitamin E) is useful in the treatment of diabetes
are its specific actions in assisting the tissues that are affected
by the blood vessel changes characteristic of the disease.
Alpha tocopheral can decrease the oxygen needed in the
tissues, it can prevent thrombosis and it can accelerate the
development of collateral (alternative) circulation. The
decrease in insulin usage in about one third of the cases is an
incidental benefit.' In this excellent book Dr Shute states that
there are over forty papers now available in medical literature
to confirm the great value of Vitamin E in the treatment of
diabetes.

Before insulin was discovered diabetics usually died in a
diabetic coma in early life. With the prescribing of insulin,
diabetics live longer, and the seriousness of the circulation
damage caused by the diabetic situation is now all too

evident. Diabetes, which was originally classed as a disorder of carbohydrate metabolism, is now seen as a disturbance of the entire cardiovascular system. Vitamin E is unique in its treatment of the diabetic complications associated with the blood and circulation.

Minerals
Although the vitamins previously discussed are all of value in the treatment of diabetes, with the exception of Vitamin B_6 and Vitamin E it cannot be said that extra vitamins are *essential* in diabetic treatment. The role of certain minerals, however, in diabetic control is more clearly defined and diabetes is one of the few diseases in which the use of supplementary minerals is of greater value than the taking of vitamins. Although many minerals are implicated in blood sugar control there are five minerals of special value to the diabetic. These are: Chromium, Magnesium, Manganese, Potassium and Zinc.

Chromium
Recent research has shown that chromium is a vital component of the Glucose Tolerance Factor (G.T.F.). This organic compound made up of chromium, Vitamin B_3 and amino acids (proteins) plays an important role in effective insulin-glucose control. Animal experimentation has shown that a certain type of rat develops diabetes with a chromium deficient diet. The blood chromium level decreases with age, with the Western diet and during pregnancy (providing a clue to the frequency of diabetes in pregnant women).

Although much research is still needed to fully understand the role of chromium and the G.T.F., it is known that humans cannot easily synthesize G.T.F. unless the intestinal bacteria are in a healthy balanced state and the diet contains adequate chromium. It has been found that the taking of glucose either orally or intravenously causes a profound fall in the blood chromium level. Virus infections also influence blood chromium with a drop of up to 60 per cent. This may explain the diabetic's poor response to infections. Although chromium occurs in many foods it is not always easily absorbed, the absorption rate being from 1-10 per cent of total chromium ingestion. Fortunately the richest source of chromium is brewer's yeast which is an easily absorbed organic form widely available and inexpensive. Chromium is also essential in the metabolism of proteins and fats, and the lack of chromium is implicated in certain eye diseases. The G.T.F. is non-toxic and appears to have a hormone-like effect, being released into the blood in response to insulin.

Magnesium

This essential mineral is frequently reduced during food processing. It is also removed from our water by water softeners, and greatly reduced in cooking. It is linked with other minerals, in particular calcium and potassium. Both of these are dependent on the presence of magnesium for their normal absorption. Deficiency of magnesium has been found in liver disease, diabetic ketosis and arteriosclerosis, and there is evidence available to link magnesium deficiency with diabetic retinopathy. Six of the nine enzymes involved with sugar metabolism need magnesium. There is enormous magnesium loss through the bladder with alcohol consumption, possibly providing a link between cirrhosis of the liver, diabetes and magnesium deficiency.

Manganese

It has been noted that diabetics have 50 per cent less manganese in their blood than do healthy subjects. This important trace mineral is essential for normal insulin output and plays a vital role in the utilization of many vitamins including Vitamin C, choline, biotin and thiamine. Manganese is also essential for the normal transmission of nerve impulses, and its deficiency may lead to many muscle-nerve problems, although a great deal of research is still needed to fully understand this aspect of manganese metabolism.

Modern farming and food processing methods deplete the manganese content of many foods.

Potassium

Whenever the body loses fluid it loses potassium. Diuretic drugs that increase urine loss, vomiting, diarrhoea and diabetes all increase potassium deficiency. Magnesium and potassium are related, and a magnesium deficiency may also produce a deficiency of potassium. Potassium influences blood sugar, for, where there is an abnormal response to the taking of glucose, potassium will frequently create a balance. For this reason it is often prescribed for the diabetic 'hypo' effect. With stress or adrenal exhaustion the body loses potassium; furthermore, the excess taking of sodium (salt) depresses potassium availability. Fortunately potassium is found in foods a diabetic should have in abundance, namely, vegetables and fruits.

Zinc

Zinc is one of the many substances that diabetics lose in their urine. It is part of the structure of insulin and is thought to influence the secretion of several other hormones. Deficiency of zinc may affect the circulation, lead to cold hands and feet, and a sure sign of zinc deficiency is the characteristic white zinc spots on the nails. Zinc is added to insulin to prolong its action, for the storage and release of insulin is enhanced in the presence of zinc. As long ago as 1938 it was demonstrated that the pancreatic tissue of diabetics contains less than 50 per cent of the zinc in the tissue of healthy control subjects.

Dr Robert Atkins, of America, describes zinc deficiency as 'the No. 1 trace mineral deficiency'. With low zinc levels in the body there may be loss of taste sense, poor wound healing, painful periods, lower resistance to infections, joint inflammation, poor memory and decreased sexual function.

Summary

The foregoing should serve to offer a superficial insight into the role of certain vitamins and minerals in the treatment of diabetes. You may ask: 'How do I know if I need these substances and where can I obtain them?' As previously stated, it would not be wise to generalize on dosages for all types of diabetic, and the need for supplements can only be accurately assessed by hair or blood analysis coupled with a detailed case history evaluation. This would indicate the need, and your practitioner would prescribe the dosages. There are many books, some of which are listed under *Recommended Reading* (see page 61) that do list specific amounts of vitamins and minerals but this is never a good substitute for individual prescribing.

Emphasis Foods
The lists of emphasis foods that follow can be utilized to recognize the vitamin and mineral-rich foods that are of specific value to the diabetic. This will ensure that by including such foods in the diet the vital nutrients listed will be amply supplied.

Vitamin-Rich Emphasis Foods
Vitamin A (Measured in USP or International Units — iu's). Found in most vegetables and fruits, especially carrots, green vegetables, tomatoes and melons; also fish, liver and lean meat.

Vitamin B_1 (Thiamine, Thiamine Chloride). Measured in milligrams — mg. Found in wheatgerm, brown rice, brewer's yeast, wheat bran, wholegrain cereals, seeds and nuts, beans, milk and milk products, leafy green vegetables and potatoes.

Vitamin B_2 (Riboflavin, Vitamin G). Measured in milligrams — mg. Found in brewer's yeast, milk, cheese, liver, tongue, wheatgerm, almonds, sunflower seeds and leafy vegetables.

Vitamin B_3 (Niacin, Nicotinic Acid, Niacinamide, Nicotinamide). Measured in milligrams — mg. Found in brewer's yeast, wheatgerm, brown rice, nuts, sunflower seeds, green vegetables, liver, lean meat, poultry and fish.

Pantothenic Acid (Vitamin B_5, Calcium Pantothenate). Measured in milligrams — mg. Found in brewer's yeast, organ meats, wheatgerm, peanuts, peas, Royal jelly, whole grain bread and cereal, green vegetables, beans and egg yolk.

Vitamin B_6 (Pyridoxine). Measured in milligrams — mg. Found in brewer's yeast, bananas, avocado, wheatgerm, wheat bran, milk, egg yolk, organ meats, liver, peanuts, walnuts, green vegetables, green peppers, carrots, pecan nuts. Raw foods contain more than cooked foods as cooking destroys Vitamin B_6.

Choline (Lipotropic factor). Measured in milligrams — mg. Found in lecithin (made from soya beans), brewer's yeast, egg yolk, fish, soya beans, cheese, sunflower seeds, comfrey leaves, kelp, bananas, peanuts, wheatgerm, liver and pollen.

Inositol. Measured in milligrams — mg. Found in lecithin, brewer's yeast, brain, heart, wheatgerm, brown rice, nuts, molasses, oatmeal, milk and citrus fruits.

Vitamin B_{12} (Cobalamin, Cyanocobalamin). Measured in

micrograms — mcg. Found in meat (especially liver), brewer's yeast, poultry, fish, eggs, cheese, sunflower seeds, comfrey leaves, kelp, bananas, peanuts, wheatgerm and pollen.

Folic Acid (Vitamin B₉, Folate, Folacin). Measured in milligrams — mg. Found in green leaves of all kinds, liver, brewer's yeast, mushrooms, nuts and wheatgerm.

Vitamin C (Ascorbic Acid). Measured in milligrams — mg. Found in citrus fruits and all fresh fruit and vegetables, especially rosehips, acerola cherries, blackcurrants, peppers and tomatoes, etc.

Vitamin E (Tocopherol, D-Alpha Tocopherol). Measured in international units — iu's or milligrams — mg (1 iu = 1 mg). Found in wheatgerm oil, all raw seeds, nuts and grains, cabbage, spinach, asparagus, broccoli, whole grain wheat, brown rice, oats and peanuts.

Mineral-Rich Emphasis Foods
Chromium (Cr). Measured in micrograms — mcg. Found in brewer's yeast, natural hard water, wheatgerm, mushrooms, liver, black pepper, beef and beer.

Manganese (Mn). Measured in milligrams — mg. Found in leafy vegetables, peas, beans, whole grains, nuts, oranges, grapefruit, bran, egg yolk and kelp.

Magnesium (Mg). Measured in milligrams — mg. Found in nuts, soyabeans, green vegetables, figs, apples, lemons, peaches, almonds, whole grains, sunflower seeds, brown rice and sesame seeds.

Potassium (K). Measured in milligrams — mg. Found in all vegetables, especially green leaves, oranges, whole grains, sunflower seeds, nuts, milk, potatoes and bananas.

Zinc (Zn). Measured in milligrams — mg. Found in wheatgerm, brewer's yeast, meat, fish, seeds, milk, whole grains, nuts, peas, mushrooms, carrots, herrings, oysters, liver, sunflower seeds, eggs and onions.

CHAPTER 7

OTHER CONSIDERATIONS

Exercise has been described as the third leg in the treatment of diabetes, after diet and medication, or insulin. Activity of all types is an essential part of blood sugar control as exercise moves blood glucose into the body's cells without needing insulin, thus conserving the insulin and reducing the diabetic's high blood sugar. Regular exercise also strengthens muscles, improves breathing, stimulates blood flow and reduces circulating fats. This is of special importance to the obese diabetic as exercise will burn more calories and speed up metabolism.

Exercise and Calories Used

Walking slowly for an hour	200 Calories
Bowling for an hour	200 Calories
Dancing for an hour	300 Calories
Gardening for an hour	300 Calories
Walking briskly for an hour	300 Calories
Cycling for an hour	600 Calories
Playing golf for two hours	600 Calories
Swimming for an hour	600 Calories
Jogging for an hour	600 Calories
Playing football for an hour	600 Calories

Two notes of caution: 1. Exercise reduces the insulin requirement and young 'brittle' diabetics may 'hypo' unless their exercise, food and insulin are all carefully controlled. 2. For the middle-aged and elderly diabetics the rule should be 'Walk, don't run'! Begin by walking, and only jog or trot after three or four weeks' exercise. This applies to any exercise or sport. Do not be too enthusiastic at first.

Smoking

Diabetics should not smoke. There are many reasons that can be summarized as follows:
1. Smoking contributes to narrow and brittle arteries which can lead to coronary thrombosis.

2. Smoking increases the blood sugar by stimulating the release of adrenalin.
3. Smoking reduces available Vitamin C to the extent of 25mg per cigarette.

Experiments in Sweden in 1965 showed that the smoke from one cigarette, even when not inhaled, can increase blood sugar levels by 36 per cent in ten minutes. Heavy smokers develop symptoms of cardio-vascular damage very similar to the elderly diabetic. To be a diabetic and to smoke is asking for trouble.

Alcohol
All alcohol drinks are high in calories. In spite of this all alcohol need not be completely banned from the diabetic's table. The controlled diabetic can quite safely take the occasional drink. There is, however, one special precaution: certain alcoholic drinks have a high sugar content. These include sweet wines, beer, champagne, liqueur, brandies and sweet Martinis. It should also be remembered that diabetics do not 'hold their drink' too well, particularly if on oral drugs, and a severe 'hypo' effect can be confused with drunkenness. The liver in diabetes is especially prone to damage. If this is suspected, alcohol should be avoided completely.

Coffee and Tea
Coffee and tea both contain caffeine which has a similar effect to sugar, and by stimulating the adrenal glands causes the blood sugar to rise. This is clearly not ideal for the diabetic. Caffeine also burns up available thiamine (Vitamin B_1) which is an essential vitamin for the diabetic. Caffeine-free coffee and herb teas are available which provide excellent substitutes for the usual coffee and tea.

Sugar Substitutes
There are two groups of substitutes that can be used in place of table sugar or sucrose. These are: Artificial sugars (i.e. cyclamates, saccharine, etc.) and Alternative sugars (i.e. zylose and fructose).

Artificial or Synthetic Sugars
Although banned in the United States (as a suspected cancer-forming substance) cyclamates are still available in Britain,

whilst saccharine is available in most countries. The three sugar alcohols, sorbitol, mannitol and xylitol, are also used in certain products. It is advisable for the diabetic to avoid all forms of artificial sweeteners. Where there is a need to follow a sugar-free diet it makes dieting considerably easier if the craving for sugar is reduced in favour of more savoury foods. Some authorities maintain that synthetic sweeteners have a sugar-like effect and do in fact trigger the pancreas into activity, rather like a conditioned reflex. This is not so strange when one considers that in some individuals even the smell or sight of food will stimulate gall bladder and stomach activity.

Alternative Sugars

Fructose (fruit sugar)

Fructose is quite safe for diabetics. The only drawback in using fructose in food is its high calorie value. It has been demonstrated that fructose acts as a buffer and steadies the rapid swings in blood sugar levels. It has also been observed that fructose assists the body to reduce blood alcohol levels, thus explaining why drinks mixed with fruit juice are less potent than other mixtures.

Xylose (wood sugar)

Although xylose occurs naturally in many fruits and vegetables its chief commercial source is wood pulp. It can be absorbed without the need for insulin, yet unlike fructose it has been found that xylose can also inhibit tooth decay. At present xylose is expensive to market, being three times more costly than sugar. It may well be that xylose will soon become the diabetic's chief sweetener.

Fibre

The subject of fibre has become very popular in recent years. Although advocated almost a century ago by naturopaths and nutritionists it is only in the last 10-15 years that the value of whole grain and fibre-rich foods has been accepted by the medical establishment. Fibre, sometimes called roughage, is not a nutrient and it provides increased bulk in our diet without greatly increased calories. It facilitates efficient bowel activity, reduces cholesterol absorption and serves to slow down the absorption of sugars from the intestines.

High fibre foods retain their vitamins and minerals, and the bulky nature of fibre ensures that our appetite control is not over-ridden as in the more highly refined, easily consumed foods. The modern refined low-fibre diet has been linked to such diverse conditions as diverticulitis, coronary heart disease, colon-rectal cancer, varicose veins and haemorrhoids, gall bladder disease and constipation. The carbohydrates are the richest source of fibre and the list below gives some idea of the main fibre-rich foods.

	Portion in grams	Fibre in grams
Apricot (fresh)	150	3.2
Beans (kidney)	60	4.4
Blackberries	150	10.9
All Bran (R)	20	5.3
Corn (sweet)	60	3.5
Figs (dried)	20	3.6
Peas (boiled)	60	7.3
Prunes (dried)	30	4.9
Raspberries (fresh)	180	13.3
Spinach (fresh)	90	5.7

Fibre is of special value to the diabetic, for meals low in fibre raise the blood sugar level higher than fibre-rich meals. The bulky fibre foods are absorbed more slowly, satisfy the appetite and have fewer calories. The valuable effect of fibre on cholesterol and triglyceride levels is a bonus to the diabetic.

Herbs and Spices
With a few reservations these valuable additions to recipes are permitted to the diabetic although of course, not in excess. The diabetic's diet, with its obvious restrictions and limitations, may at times become dull and uninteresting, and the judicious use of selected herbs and spices should therefore have a special value. For a very comprehensive description of the various herbs and spices, the book by Elizabeth Russell Taylor called *The Diabetic Cookbook* is of particular value.

Salt
Food flavour is obviously essential for food enjoyment but
the main seasoning, salt, is often forbidden the diabetic, for
many diabetics have heart problems, high blood pressure,
eye problems and kidney conditions. However, low sodium
salts are available from Health Food Stores and these may be
safely used.

Pickles, etc.
Other condiments and flavourings that are permitted include
onions, garlic, cider-vinegar, mustard, pickles and pepper. It
should be remembered, however, that mustard and most
pickles contain a certain amount of sugar and salt. A visit to
your local Health Food Store should provide useful
information on available low sugar mayonnaise, relishes,
pickles, etc.

GLOSSARY

Acidosis   Said to occur when the compensatory mechanisms of overbreathing and creation of very acid urine are 'stretched to the limit' and drowsiness or coma occur. Ketone substances are present in the blood.

Adrenal Glands   Paired glands, also called the suprarenal glands, located adjacent to the tip of each kidney.

Brittle Diabetes   This is a condition in which young insulin-dependent diabetics with a very sensitive glucose-insulin balance are easily upset by stress, exercise or wrong eating.

Endocrine   Means, literally, secreted internally. Applied to substances produced and released into the blood, especially hormones.

Emphasis Foods   Foods of special value to diabetics owing to their vitamin/mineral rich content.

Enzymes   Substances produced by the body, acting as a catalyst by increasing reactions of various substances.

'Hypo' Effect   Hypoglycaemia produced in the diabetic patient owing to excess insulin dosage or insufficient carbohydrate intake.

Ketogenic Diet   High fat/protein diet: prescribed to encourage weight loss through breakdown of body's fat reserves.

Ketosis   See *Acidosis*.

Pituitary Gland   Master gland situated in skull. Produces substances that influence thyroid, adrenals, growth, gonads and fluid balance.

Saturated Fats Predominantly animal fats: these fats are usually solid with carbon bonds filled with hydrogen.

Triglycerides Stored body fat; derived from the diet or synthesized in the liver.

Unsaturated Fats Predominantly vegetable liquid oils which may be converted into solid fat by hydrogenation.

RECOMMENDED READING

Diabetes by James W. Anderson (Martin Dunitz)

The Diabetic Cookbook by Elizabeth Russell Taylor (Hamlyn)

Low Blood Sugar by Martin L. Budd (Thorsons)

Speaking of Diabetes by Petzoldt and Schöffling (Delair Publishing, New York)

How to Get Well by Paavo Airola (Health Plus Publishers, Phoenix, Arizona, U.S.A.)

Nurtition and Vitamin Therapy by Michael Lesser (Thorsons)

Recipes for Diabetics by Billie Little (Bantam Books)

The Saccharine Disease by T. L. Cleave (Wright, Bristol)

Dr Atkins Nutrition Breakthrough by R. C. Atkins, M.D. (Bantam Books)

The Vegetarian on a Diet by Margaret Cousins and Jill Metcalfe (Thorsons)

Cooking for Diabetes by Jill Metcalfe (Thorsons)

INDEX